little terrarium

Hannah Fries

Hedgerow Books
AMHERST, MASSACHUSETTS

Copyright © 2016 by Hannah Fries

Cover art © Madeline von Foerster, *Specimen Cabinet*, 2008, 12 x 16 in., oil and egg tempera on panel

Cover design by Carolyn Eckert.

All rights reserved, including the right of reproduction in whole or in part in any form.

Printed and published by
Hedgerow Books of Levellers Press
Amherst, Massachusetts

For Oma, who always knew

CONTENTS

Among the Ruins

Naming the Trees · 3
Pomegranate · 5
Noah's Wife · 6
Svalbard Global Seed Vault · 9
Fugal Prayer · 10
Almost Easter · 14
Mary · 15
But See · 17
Seashell of the Paper Fig (*Ficidae*) · 18
Love at Formel's Junkyard · 19
How to Use a Hook · 21
Sillage de la Reine · 22
Burlesque · 23
Pygmalion's Girl · 24
House Plant · 26
Potatoes · 27
Mandala · 29
Next · 30

Sea Paintings: Winslow Homer (1836–1910)

The Artist's Studio in an Afternoon Fog · 33
The Berry Pickers · 34
Inside the Bar, Cullercoats · 37
The Fog Warning · 39
Fox Hunt · 40
The Life Line · 43
West Point, Prout's Neck, Maine · 44

Metamorphoses

The Wedding at Cana · 49
It Is Not Enough · 51
Genealogy · 52
Three Girls · 54
Operculum · 55
Early Morning · 56
A Life Inside of This One · 57
Midnight Baking · 58
Descending Killington Peak · 59
Bloom · 60
Orb Weaver (*Nephila*) · 61
Night Crawlers · 62
A Girl Restored to Life · 63
Recipe for Resurrection · 64
Winter Wren · 65
Epithalamion · 67
Manna, Honeydew · 68

Notes · 69
Acknowledgments · 71

But how can we hope to save ourselves in that which is most fragile?
— ITALO CALVINO

little terrarium

Among the Ruins

Naming the Trees

We are trying to name the trees as we walk—
                        early spring, no help from leaves,
though their shapes are etched on our minds, branching
      like my hand against your chest.
Only the texture of bark: smooth, riveted, peeling,
                and their crowns: spreading or drooping;
         needles in groups of three
                  or five, or soft fronds.

We name them because they tower over us, here
                where they were logged, burned,
where they marched back anyway
            across charred slopes, saplings
        cracking rain-pocked earth. Moosewood,
musclewood, white ash.
              We are naming the trees

that edge the perimeter of the burnt-out factory where sky
      shouts through windows
                on one wall left standing—
letters rubbed out from caving sides—
      a wood treatment plant hidden behind barbed wire's
             curtain of honeysuckle: what strangles
    the forest undoes us too.
              We are naming,
we are naming the trees before they walk away

because we are unlearning forgetfulness,
                taking our time,
and right now time loves us
         because we just made love, late this morning, slowly

waking each other up, ribbons of light
        streaming in on our bodies, through branches,
through blinds, and then
              we got up and went outside to name the trees:
horse chestnuts, magnolia, tight-budded crab apple,
                                  thinking pink.

On the back of your hand, too, blue veins branch
              like roots seeking water,
      like the river that roils under the bridge we cross
          to a place farther along,
where we can fish, not think
              toxic silt carried downstream.
Think: tree swallows in silver maples. We press
      our hands against bark to print its pattern on our palms.

   I say
your name, and you turn
         like a stem toward light. I love you.
There is no good reason
              why any of this should be. Today
we are naming the trees, calling them back.
     Shagbark hickory, tamarack,
                black cherry.
Sugar maple, we say, and it is on our tongues:

                    Tap it now, in March,
   the ground a mash of snow and mud, sap rising
from the roots, a clear drop on the finger:
      small sweetness we taste because we know it's there.

Pomegranate

The immodest blush, firm swell,
flared navel of the flower's dead end—

from what black bough was it pulled,
from what spreading tree
on what busted hillside pocked

with hurt. Afghanistan, Iraq.
Pakistan and Iran, your burnt

orchards, shrouded and sick.
Fruit of the underworld,
fruit of life. Peel back

the stubborn outer pulp,
milky underside, filament clinging

to garnet drops, glassy
little hearts of bursting: *granatum*:
grenade. Crimson

spray on the child's tongue and hand.
A long drink in the constricted

throat—grenadine,
half sweet, half
gone. The fastest-holding stain.

Noah's Wife

So I've started to gather seeds,
stitch them
into the hem of my robe,

a dozen flowers
in the cuff of my sleeve.

**

Rain: small craters in the dust
as if for holes to plant the wheat.
Refreshing at first.
Things will want to grow.

**

My ankles blacken
with mud. Sheep sink
to their knees, bleating.

Cruel, to choose.

**

The beasts, obedient, file in.
Who will save the olive and the barley?
I keep a cherry stone beneath my tongue.

**

When the bears shamble in with burs
in their coats, I rejoice.
I pluck their coarse fur clean.

**

The giraffes are seasick — knobby
legs wobble beneath their bellies.

So am I. I pick through
feces for seeds of the last fruit
they ate.

**

The raven sits on my shoulder.
I feel his beak in my hair, and
his feathers are oil.
He follows me, my shadow's
shadow of wings.
I should have been left out there
in the sheeting rain.

**

The clouds have dried
and withered like my hands.

Mountain peaks are islands, thrashed and bare.

The water is so still: a bowl
filled with sky.

**

Two snakes have bred.
Their young slither about the floor.
I think of the poppy seeds sewn
into my right sleeve, a constellation
shifting around my wrist.

**

The dove is a fool: it returns
to this mess of wood and flesh.

The raven went out first—
seeds tucked in his smoke-black beak.

He won't return.
He'll fly until he's through.

Svalbard Global Seed Vault

The mountain, body of sandstone and ice,
quakes with the blast of a long tunnel,
        opening into echoes of vaulted rooms.
Seeds, sleeping children,
                come to dream in the cold,
not by wind or wing, but wrapped
        and sealed, unopened,
like the still-fresh honey in an Egyptian tomb —
        a promise for the next world.

Some will survive a hundred years, or thousands:
        the Aztecs' amaranth and maize,
Thailand's long-grained Japonica,
                black-purple as thunder.
Apples from Kazakh forests, buckwheat from Siberia,
        quinoa culled from the Andes' heights.
And minuscule teff,
whose name means "lost" in Amharic — so small,
        it vanishes from your palm.
Sometimes famine comes that fast.

And if there is no one left
        to come for them, what then?
Through the doubt-filled drought of night,
        the seeds go on
                dreaming of dampness, sun —
the mustard seed, hushed
        kingdom, waits inside its yellow globe.

Fugal Prayer

I.

Hear the fugue our engines chant, grinding
gears, discordant: the world that eats itself,
that throws its bloody subject
to the sky, is surprised (why?)
to hear *God* echoed back,
a stranger's voice, drowning its own
cry before it finishes — unlistening, the world
       that eats its anger
                retches it, bitter, out.

What is this answer, our own
              voices ringing in our ears?
We take it for mocking
              and shout again.

Try this for a subject, try this, says the rain
all night repeating against
the pane, try this, repeating against my self, stripped
and exposed and eyelids   (mocking, repeating)
twitching in sleep, flesh peeled back while armies
march deserts, march my ribs' white ridges,
        press their weapons against each other
and bruise me.

Try this, God. But God, You
              tried this, flesh, ribs,
      Your own: he wept.

II.

An episode for Your pages:
the man on the street, he wept,
blight on the bench of a well-
off town. Stubble-cheeked,
rough-palmed, he
took my hand and asked
my name, showing his,
tattooed between
forefinger and thumb.
I gave it to him,
but nothing else.
*You are very kind, very
kind,* he said.

III.

I gave him nothing, no counterpoint
 to this devouring—engines chant
and the world eats itself, flesh over
ribs, the starved, and the soul inside
its little terrarium. (This is another voice,
 buried but trying.)
 I would keep it here,
eager, contained, but leaves press the slick
sides, tear-dropped with condensation, their own
pale breath. Green veined faces against
moist glass: Try this,
they cry, try this: the sky, throbbing
all night and rain that mists over hot
peeled skin—nerves shining.

        It is too late to keep this green thing
safe, it has broken out. It stretches around
the cold room, wants
to wrap its shivering vines around it all.

I have given myself up, let it go, I could lose
it all in a frost.

IV.

        An answer?
Is an echo
        an answer?

Rain and the rustling of leaves.

V.

God, this fugue the engines play, the confusion,
the grand noisy rustling, the same theme over-
        lapping. The last
                of something, again.

And don't we always love too late?

Give me at least the tragic chance, the
Dear God what have I done.
                I've nailed
the best of my self to a cross (ribs,
heaving), then knelt to weep
        (he wept) at the empty tomb at dawn.

                    Nothing but white
that morning, the linens, the absence a space.

What have I done: a hole
          and they all fall in, the sour kiss, the armies
of my ribs fall in, fall
into that cold room, and the leaves reach
out (they have broken out), their sweet green
faces, tearable, tender,
          tearing, in tattered pieces. Hold them.

VI.

Won't I kneel, won't I

bend over Earth's last flower, last fungus
ringed with flame?

Bloodied shout, eating anger.
               Very kind, he said, a whisper.

And: *Let me wash your feet.*

Almost Easter

Beneath a stone moved
by winter's plow, a crocus—
curled under, trying to get out,

a blind shove toward sun, contortions
against the dead dull weight above.
It should have been a purple cup,

or glowing white like the risen lily—
not this other white, of pale things cloistered
underground, larvae and maggots,

bones and ghosts, the white of a limb
freshly naked from its cast.
I moved the rock, I let it out.

Saved, it lived but never
stood: twisted and spent, accustomed
to beating against the dark.

Mary

No priest, no holy man ever expected
it would take a woman who bleeds.

I tow them behind me

like dogs behind the butcher,
their noses stuffed with my scent.

What to do? they asked.
Make her untouchable,

*clean as the Sabbath, sweeter
than the living can stand. Empty*

*as the pitcher she carries to the well,
that knows its emptiness only as*

the shape of water, poured in.
I am none of that.

First I resisted, as the beginning
drew near, the weight of it

over me like the pressure of sky
before a sand storm. I was afraid

to lose myself.
Even then I knew: I

was made of a yearning
the whole desert — its rushing

sweep of sky and blowing dunes,
all the uncountable grains — could not fill.

Those fluttering tongues of flame, white-hot
wings against my skin,

the searing away at the surface, that heat
I turned to more ravenously

than the body allows, like the night-
blooming flower — all mouth:

I tell you, I devoured it.

I am greedy, I would keep
for myself this flesh of my flesh,

this rapture: what fills me
tears me open.

You will be offered bread.
You will not know how to eat it.

But see

how an orchid is made to look like sex.
        The tachinid fly lands on a leaf to flash
                her private parts, opening
        and closing to catch the sun.
No wonder her mate ravishes
the flower whose petals are extended wings.
        So what if I sweep up my hair
                to show off my neck, so what
        if someone begins to kiss it?
Consider the bowerbird, jewelling
his nest with sapphire, ask the snakes braiding
        their muscled lengths. See how God is in love
                with sex, and how we are made
        in God's image! Haven't you, like a lovesick
ungulate, forgotten to eat for weeks?
Have you heard the barred owls scream
        all night? Seen fireflies flashing silent sirens?
                The woodcock spirals higher, then
        plummets in zigzags, wind
whistling through his wings.
Nothing, after all, is solid — atoms flying
        in all directions, ocean currents plunging
                into themselves. Why not two bodies
        by firelight, stunned by their bare
skin, their own flickering sudden
perfection? No hellfire here.
        When galaxies collide, there is no wreck,
                no blazing crash of suns and moons,
        just a rushing together, a folding in —
and a heat beyond orchids —
birthing, baptizing heat.

Seashell of the Paper Fig (*Ficidae*)

I want to be found
before I am broken.

There's no other risk.
I hide conspicuously

among the mangroves'
shady fingers — white.

Pick me up: see
how wide I open,

translucent, filled
with your palm's pink light.

Love at Formel's Junkyard

When I say, Formel's is where Celibacy went to die,
I mean the name of my late '84 Chevy.
You couldn't pick up anyone in that ride,
which is why I like to imagine parking
at the junkyard — steaming the windows
of a stalled-out station wagon, springs
bruising your back, as you breathe hard
the smell of mildew — while outside fenders gleam
in the moonlight by mountains of tires.
Lovemaking among the ruins. "Muskrat Love"
on the radio. In seventh grade spin-the-bottle,
we lunged across the circle, smashing
our tight mouths together. Embarrassing, that desire
to grab, to pull back quick enough to keep
oneself intact. We only wanted to delay
what we suspected but couldn't say:
someday we'd each come to pieces
in somebody else's arms. Take
the patron saint of Siena, Santa Caterina,
ministering during the plague, when construction
on the cathedral ceased for lack of living hands.
She fell from a high window and lived —
a tiny cross engraved on the piazza stair
where she landed. They say she received the stigmata,
but, for humility's sake, it didn't appear till after death.
Even a saint is allotted just so many miracles. Her head
is there, in the church, behind shadowed glass.
Press a button to lend it dim light: outline of sunken cheeks —

so you have to squint, so the grotesque maintains
its holy proportions. Her finger, too, shriveled and thin,
eternally points to heaven, or to the rest
of her body, somewhere in Rome.
Everyone wants a piece of the sacred: the divvied-up saint,
the girl who dodges the bottle every time, or maybe
a few minutes in the moonlit junkyard—unattainable beauty
you rip apart by wanting too badly. Orpheus
torn to pieces. In Corot's painting of Eurydice, she sits
alone on a rock with her snake-bitten ankle. Tenderly,
she looks at the wound, venom already begun to slide
through braided veins. Her face is sad, but
almost smiling, as though she sees in the swelling holes
a vision of everything to come:
her lover's severed head taken up by the river,
muskrats on the banks like an ad hoc chorus, and the reeds
bending to hear the tongue still make a murmured song.

How to Use a Hook

Wait for the pink proboscis to emerge
alien-like from its head, four hooked pincers
blind and gnashing. If you are quick enough,
cut it clean off. This is what she's learned,
eleven years old, ponytail, jean shorts
and skinny legs. She keeps her fingers
out of the way because nothing appreciates
going from predator to bait, this bloodworm
no exception, writhing as she pins the creamy body,
its dark bloodline, to the planks of the dock,
and when she cuts its jaws it spills deep red,
as if she'd cut her own finger.
Small frown, tongue between her lips, she sticks
her hook into the severed end and eases the metal
through until she has a hook-shaped worm,
a slimy knot over the barbed end, her fingers
sticky with blood and ooze, mud jammed under her nails.
This, she knows, is how you catch a striper, the silver sheen
she'll glimpse before it escapes, or, with luck,
she'll hold. Another kink at the end of the hook,
and she lets the tail hang limp now, barely twitching.
She rinses her hands, stands, flips the bail, and,
hooked worm dangling over sunburnt shoulder,
flings the bloody mess as far as it will go.

Sillage de la Reine
> —*a perfume reconstructed from the notes of Marie-Antoinette's chief perfumer*

Rhizomes from a Tuscan iris
cured five years, jasmine,
orange blossom, tuberose
(bergamot to lighten the head),
a perfect blend for a lover
of gardens and soft intensity,
petals' sticky uncurling
in sunshine's glaze.
It hides all things rank:
the stench of open sewers
beyond the walls, the unwashed
body—burn what remains (woody
essence of sandalwood and cedar),
set this scent as a flame
in the laden air. Wear it,
if you can bear to break
the seal (base notes
of Tonkin musk, gray amber),
see how passing lips
will tremble to brush your neck,
see what desires
to be swallowed by sweet things,
see if it tempts the blade.

Burlesque

On the stage, which you can see quite well from your seat
by the door near the bouncer who let you sneak in free,

a woman in a lobster suit, bright red
and ridiculously burdened, begins to dance, peeking

between her huge claws and waving them in sensuous loops,
turning to show off her tail before she starts to take herself apart—

a piece of shell, a claw, one left to coyly cover her breasts,
then not—each time sweeping a newly naked,

pale piece of her through flecks of gold confetti
that stick to the sweat on her skin: here, you realize,

the joke becomes flesh, white and pierceable,
because she is not entirely beautiful, not thin or fit, and you,

watching, try to imagine yourself under the hot lights,
whether you'd have it in you to fling off the last piece of costume

with a flourished arc that extends from your imperfection,
to dip yourself not gracefully but gloriously in the glittering butter.

Pygmalion's Girl

I.

I had no childhood, did not grow
into my body — but emerged,
whole, from a man's imagination.

You might say I'm lucky to be crafted
by my husband because he is bound to worship me,
or if he sees any flaw, it is his own and of his making.

I think, when he holds me,
how he carved my breasts to fit his hand,
brushed the dust from my tiny nipples,

ran his tongue around them for good measure.
He gave me a navel I had no use for,
and the dust collected there

as he worked my hips, gripped
the bones of my pelvis.
He made my feet too small,

so I teeter when I walk.
The first time I stood, I toppled
into his stunned embrace.

II.

It is not pleasant to remind a man of his shortcomings
who once thought he could mold perfection.

I thank the goddess, not him, for shaping me
a voice to say, *I am flesh now, not stone.*

At first, when I spoke, he startled, pulled away,
but I have learned to weave

melodies out of air. While he grows still
and soft with sleep, while his breathing slows,
I braid them in constant variation.

III.

After he'd carved my blank white eyes,
he brought me trinkets and silk — I saw them
as from a depth of water. Wavy and rippled
above the surface, his love-addled face.
When I think how it is to *become*,
that is, to make oneself, I think
of water, always shifting shape.
Could I not, having gone from stone
to flesh, go next from flesh to water,
trilling over rocks, in time boring out
deep holes so flawlessly round, glittering,
slipping through his hands.

House Plant

The man at the nursery told you
I could live in a closet.
It depends what you call living.
Meaning, you could leave me
        unwatered while you are away.
Meaning, I'll always be green for you,
        because that is my disposition.

He didn't think you'd try it, but you
were curious because you thought
        I lived for light.
I do. I turn to it, lean for it, stretch
        in any direction, whichever way
I am rotated, whatever dark corner
you stand me in. I'll find it. Call it.

What I do with this darkness
        is my experiment. Your old
shoes. Ghostly skins of your shirts.
I am slivered and spindly-legged,
        spring-loaded and
yes, still green, a strange green,
waiting for the shadows of your feet.

You have forgotten me,
        but he was right. I can
slice this starved space
        with the tip of a tendril.
I can break my own heart with any
        blade of light
that edges through the bottom of that door.

Potatoes

Maggie is telling me about her past lives
that burst through the surface of her days
like fish from a still pond.
We are digging potatoes in her garden,
plunging our hands deep into the cold
soil of early October. Plumes of fog
on the river, early sun scattering on snapdragons,
cosmos, seedpods of love-in-a-mist.
Do you have nightmares here? she asks,
as we feel for lumpy clusters,
working our fingers around
their circumferences to pry them out
because the shovel has sliced too many
already, so we are on our knees, fingernails
turning black—*something happened here*,
she says, and shudders. Stares at her hands
like they're stained with something other
than damp soil. *I was a little girl, a little
girl my entire life… and lived alone,
with my father… a cabin in the woods. I knew you then—*
she stares at me—*I just don't know how.* I don't know
what to say when she talks like this, when she starts to slip
into an intensity I can't touch, and I want to drag her
out of the swampy past, the one where I couldn't
save her, and dunk her in the river, press
a fistful of herbs to her face. Potatoes come up
like gold in a sieve, still skinned with dirt
but unmistakable—I spit on one and rub out
the mud: deep purple. Maggie's wide dark eyes.
She reminds me of a childhood friend,
kindergarten, the girl with the serious face
and the outie bellybutton who lifted her t-shirt

to show me: little nubbin on her smooth tummy—
it made me laugh, and she pulled her shirt back down
and held it there. But I wanted to see it again,
to touch that evidence of inversion, how
the inside can sometimes rise up and leave
itself exposed. I thought if I could grab
that knot and pull it, she might turn
inside-out, a shiny open tulip, red
and overbloomed, petals sprawled in a circle
of dangerous backbends around a deep brown
center. I have climbed down into the round sunken
room called a *kiva* in the Anasazi ruins—
in the center, a small hole in the soft stone,
sipapu, bellybutton of a people, where the ancestors
first emerged into the present world. Through what
hole they left again, or why, is not clear. Half-
ground corn in a smooth depression. The cliffs
resound with whispers, like the ones Maggie hears
rising out of the earth when she finds herself
in a place she has seen in a dream and it begins
to tell her stories and her body aches
with another life's beating. I don't know how
to pull her through to where we are
still kneeling in the dirt, because she is telling me
of a forest that covered this field, a cabin and a stick
by the door and someone is coming. *I remember
you,* she says—and I see myself
hiding behind the door as she steps toward the anger
that crashes in, and our buckets are full of potatoes
tumbling from the edges, my hands stiff
and cracked from the cold, and I want to stop
now, but she keeps digging, wrenching more
from their loamy dark beds and piling them up,
little fists, clenched and knobby and strange.

Mandala

One Chinese brother could drink the ocean
and hold it in, goes the tale, but only
just so long. Colored plastic churns
in the Pacific gyre, storm-gathered, broken.

And the albatross, too, drinks waves,
feeds bright bits to her chick
on the bottle-strewn shore. The chick's body
is a mandala, symmetrically knit.

Soft down, wind-stripped, eyes eaten,
skin, weathered gone. Bones, brittle,
crack, and all gives back, gives way,

but this: plastic signature
in the gut's place—the mandala's
inverse, splayed—the undoing that persists.

Next

I'm on my way to the bar and it's raining.
My favorite shop window displays doorknobs, handles,
brass and porcelain, twisted wrought iron.
One like the latch to a child's playhouse:
inside, his collection of stones. One like the crystal
knob turned by the mother, revealing the bathroom

and the body, his opened wrists, the bright white tub.
This spring the blueberry bushes bloomed early,
froze, and never fruited. A glacier groaned, calved,
undid itself. Roadside bombs. Today is my birthday.
The storm drain's grate is open, and a truck with a hose
sucks at the hole. My friend at the bar sobs into her rum.

Later, midnight, and the sky has almost cleared,
so I drive out of town, to the field, to watch the Perseids.
Each star soaks up its space: once a minute, one rips
through, a brief crack in the dark. Through what
midnight hall do we stumble and grope for a switch
or a knob? Or better: find the doorway edged in light,
the dim sign that someone came through before.

Sea Paintings: Winslow Homer
(1836–1910)

The Artist's Studio in an Afternoon Fog

The artist's mother, hours before he's born,
stands before her easel in a wide, white,
streaked pinafore, a weather-beaten sail,
brush suspended briefly, midair. Outside
the window, the sun finds its way through
and the child inside her stirs, as if to sense
already his form within its envelope
of light (and soon, a shock, the untouched air).
Light, yes, and wisps of shadow, and, just
beginning, the shapes of things, like a scene
through fog of familiar objects made strange,
their edges just emerging: a small room,
its slanted roof, a chimney, finding themselves
vaguely, like ideas not yet quite formed.

The Berry Pickers

A man who wants to be an artist should
never look at pictures. How do you learn
the shifting shape of wind, its rare summer
sweetness, mornings when sun and rising fog
wash the sky's crisp face with a whitened sheen?
The children crouch in salt-licked shrubs,
heads down, their shoulders sun-warm and fingers
staining purple, a few tongues stained, too,
the thought of pie. The breeze is a child, shy
thing for a day. It finds the red ribbon
of a girl's hat, catching it like a kite tail
that flutters toward the hint of song perched
on a gray branch—more suggestion of bird
than bird, tiny brushstroke in the broad sky.

Inside the Bar, Cullercoats

Apron blooming in the wind, a jib, she'd
fly wing and wing if let unmoored
from the stolid rock, left foot jutting
toward the waves, hand on a hip,
and at her throat a red scarf like a life
welled up against its gray backdrop.
Behind her the boat takes her profile, stiff
billow braced for the sea's thrash but less
sure than she, on this spit of rock, waiting
for the catch — blank waters at her back,
at her feet a steely pool that holds her
shadow, left by the tide. Wide sweep
of storm clouds. On her arm hangs a basket
to catch what diminished light seeps through.

The Fog Warning

Waves black-green, ink-wet and knived, bile
in the gut of some blind beast, troughs deep,
glint on the reckless crests that thrust
the dory's nose toward the sky that closes
in with a whisper too low, too close
to the ear, and far away the schooner's
blot of sail like an uncertain home. But no
room here in the dory for melodrama:
a pair of firm hands on the oars, slicker
dark as the sea. Over the shoulder a glance
prolonged to take in distance, danger.
Stern heavy with the huge white flounder's
flank, tailfin breeching gunwale, gleaming
flesh—unlucky one from the other side.

Fox Hunt

The fox is belly-deep, rust red streak
in the drift of snow that takes its color
from everything in order to hold every
thing against it—a few prickly stems
proffering berries like drops of blood
to the fox's extended paw. Hunted,
he is for a moment paused, neck not
outstretched to speed the flight, but raised,
head turned and black ears pricked
toward the surf where it shatters over rocks,
blue-green foam, gray ocean sucking back
into sky. He turns his head but keeps
his course along the shore while faceless
crows—a jeer of black wings—wait.

The Life Line

The ship, lost ghost of comfort, loose sails
and shrouds flapping, is a splinter
among the rocks. Even the squared, razored
cliffs will be beaten in time. But now, strung
on the lifeline between, a body stolen
from ruin, one hand on the rope, the other
hanging over a jagged wave — soaked clothes
cling to thighs, breasts, soft-shaped and rippable
flesh. Spray erupts, explodes, the rescuer all
but hidden, his broad arm across her waist,
as the red rag of her scarf whips across
his face — flag in the wind to match her lips,
it renders her alone here, suspended
over the heaving deep, that taut line so thin.

West Point, Prout's Neck, Maine

Reckless precision, pull and layered flow
of paint: the force that forms the wave drives it
ceaselessly to shore. He holds it in his hand,
presses his own will against it: crimson
streak across the horizon, sunset tingeing
the ocean as it plunges at the rocks,
gets dragged between them, all churn and rush,
into the hollow body of the next
rearing wave. What to make of it,
arched back like a broken wrist, tethered
by a brush to its shattering and wild against
last light, bursting into sculpture, impossibly
paused—a salty spume of chiseled shards,
an unhinged slap to the flushed sky.

Metamorphoses

The Wedding at Cana

i.

Little it matters, drunk as we are,
when the grape-red seep
overtakes the water—
so sweet, so full to the brim,
the passed bottle, our hearts, our shoes
sloshing as we dance.

ii.

Paper birds my sisters fold
with their certain fingers, sharpening
beaks, creasing and
stretching each wing
to the position of flight:
hung with string, they stir
with a puff of laughter.

iii.

Should I grieve my solitude?
Imagine my body
like a rising crescent,
its singular thought
a clean, bright arc.

iv.

The gathered flowers
lift their fiery faces.

Even the music turns
deep garnet
like the backs of our tongues,
and we sing.

v.

Imagine the curve of my body asleep
beside another. Edges
draw in — exhalations
in the silk night air —
a silver oxbow,
contained.

vi.

Children refuse to be tired,
twirling, cheeks like poppies —
in their wake, birds
flutter, flames flicker.

vii.

That the first miracle should be
one of abundance, overflow,
glasses filled and filled — yes, open
wide the door, call in
the outside stranger.
Wind here. Wine.
Something to make us quiver.

It Is Not Enough

This is all your fault,
such desperation—my becoming
mortal—when, before,
I lived in my own wilderness,
letting birds tangle in my hair.
Loneliness was a tune I hummed
as I walked among the trees.
In that untouched present, I could save things,
make mossy beds for the small and wounded,
pull them back.
That was Eden, before you
arrived, whistling and plucking apricots,
remarking at their soft, cleft skin.
I ate, and then

that dark mouth yawned wide.
I am sadder now, but not less happy.

Crawl inside me, love, and let me
keep you here, contained.
You and all the things of our place:
owl who interrupts our nights,
fawn who nibbles our new apple trees,
and the apple trees, and the tiny unbelievable
frog who sits in the hydrangea's
white cup. Come, there's room.

Darling, I'd drink the creamy smear
of stars above our house to hold them in,
to stop the earth from tipping.

Genealogy

The red tugboat, the water wheel, and the sponges
    grown out of capsules congregate
        around the drain as the water goes. I stand

on the bathmat, wrinkled and pink, rocking to the push
    and pull of my mother's hands as they work
        me over with oil, neck to foot, sliding

down each arm and leg as though she draws
    them out of me afresh, remolding me,
        checking each knobby elbow, each

frowning knee. And sure enough, I am
    of a piece, a small pool glistening
        in the hollow of my navel—clear

as the vernal pools I explore in the strip
    of woods between our house and the neighbors',
        where, after a good rain, I wade in rubber boots

through sunken mats of leaves, looking
    for salamanders. When I step too deep,
        I love the way the water

waterfalls over the tops of my boots.
    My mother shows me princess pines—tiny
        trees that don't grow up. When she pulls

the base of one to show how a single hidden
    root connects them each to each,
        they bow and quiver, and I feel

    the cord between us, long gone
            but for the scar it left and the force it holds
                        beneath the surface. Her father, my grandfather,

constructs intricate family trees, lines
            branching, joining, dead-ending, somehow resulting,
                      finally, in my name: Old Testament standard,

echoing the names of great-grandmothers, names
            scattered through any lichen-aged graveyard.
                      When he dies, his ashes are returned still warm,

like beach sand, and the minister's surprise, when he lays
            his hand on the box, makes us laugh, relief quaking through us
                      from the heat of that dust—life in it yet.

Three Girls

But they always let us go, didn't they,
let us wade into the rippled fingers of the river
or the pressing body of the sea, our bodies
sleek, tan-lined and shin-scraped,
soles the color of clay.
We bruised our bony hips
and bottoms, tore our bathing suits
on rocky shoots of mountain rivers
where we bumped in the current
till our teeth chattered,
tumbled and ground in the North Atlantic
like sea glass against the sandy floor.
We came up burned and choking,
grew blue together.
That rip tide, that roiling crush,
tried to claim us back, numbed
first our toes, the creeping cold settling
in our cores until we dug into the hot beach,
ran like mad to shake it off,
went back for more.

Operculum

On the beach's salt-rubbed back I found
a moon snail's door, translucent,
paper-light, and faintly whirled—
snails I used to rescue as a child,
flinging those still tightly shut with life
back at the shrinking tide. Now, this

stray piece, unattached. The slick white
muscle that pulled into its home
and sealed the opening with this shield
is no doubt shriveled—gull food—
the battered shell abandoned,
a blind and concentrated eye.

Once, not even my humming loosened
what a breath now flicks away:
flimsy keepsake, stand-in for all the things
I couldn't save, dried and stinking on the shore—
a brittle door with nothing to hold in,
nothing to place itself between.

Early Morning

sometimes you wonder
>   *do I exist*

you feel like the fog on the valley floor
>   that will disappear by noon

a shape like a deer
>   on the opposite side of the field

grief settles and lifts
>   settles and lifts

sometimes it beads on your skin
>   condensing

covers you like that
>   because you are solid

and soft
>   and warm

A Life Inside of This One

God and I are alone inside a shell,
like putting your ear to a conch
to hear the sea, but instead
you *are* the conch, and all there is
is the sea, rushing like blood
in the veins of your ears.

No one knows I am here.
I am sweeping the floor, or
paying the cashier (our fingers brush),
I am cooking dinner for two.
Inside the shell, I am
climbing the long spiral while God
leans in like the pressure of the deep.
I am peeling an orange,
tying a child's shoe.

Some days, I am still; some days
I hurry, as if God were not
the soft insistent light around me,
blushing from the shell's curved walls.

I stand in an alabaster abbey,
feeling sunset sift from upper windows,
Outside, susurrus of olive trees. Within,
voices of monks in hidden chambers,
vespers filling the wide, arched room.

Midnight Baking

She makes bread while the town sleeps.
Not in the hours before dawn
when real bakers work, but late.

Outside it snows.
Her apron is snowed with flour.
In her hair too, flour,

which turns it softly gray.
She would choose to age like this,
quietly, pressing her hands

into soft dough, turning, folding,
pressing again until it begins to resist
and hold its shape.

The one she loves is asleep.
Even the bakers are sleeping now.
The dough rises through their dreaming,

and the deep night lifts
just a little as it leavens—
yeast, pungent before baking,

and the baking,
that scent of fullness finding
every corner of the house.

Descending Killington Peak

We step from darkly clustered spruce
into birch — pink and white,
bark peeled into sunrise like sloughed skin.
And though it is raining,
it is as if a shattered sun, golden leaves,
falls in shards through the gray
October sky to glow around us.

In this quiet, this shine
that comes from beneath the surface
on which we live out our lives,
I am searching for traces, from tree
to tree in the rose-gold light, some
sign that says *this is the turning,
this is how you'll know—*

Omen or rune, intimation that *this is the sweet
beginning, this is how it will end*. But
there is only the sound of our walking
muffled by what has fallen,
and we take it for what it is, layers
of glimmer and decay.

Bloom

Picasso is painting with light,
drawing a bull in air
the way a child scrawls
his name with a sparkler.
For a split second it hangs,
as any moment might.

A peony before it opens
is a fat, sticky globe.
Ants feast on its nectar
as if it hasn't already planned
to unstick itself and flare:
asking to be plucked,
pink little hand around
the flower's throat—
sweet and cloying, the smell
of infants, edge of the bodily—
unpetaling into a pool of rot.

The bloom of everything—
our seams and fusions,
the hips we birth from, folds
of time and space—
unravels. All those dark
chasms widen. We wave
at the glint of what's familiar
across the black distance.

The artist crouches where he's finished,
eyes raised, seeing it disappear.

Orb Weaver (*Nephila*)

Five times the tensile strength of steel,
        golden when sun-touched,
these spider webs were gathered by fishermen
        and thrown out on the sea (strange glints
in the shallows) to catch a writhing shimmer —
        the makers palm-sized, long legs
angled like a cross.

Imagine spider-catchers, women
        with bamboo poles, flicking
the females from three-foot webs,
        placing each in a tiny
harness, twenty-four at a time, to draw,
        slowly, from trembling bodies,
yards of their life's filament

then wound on reels and spun
        into silken thread. A textile
woven from a million arachnids' undoing,
        glows in a museum now. And they,
the imprisoned ones, held until empty,
        were set free to try again
their own art, if they had it in them.

A grasshopper, and then — unlikely catch — a small
        bird flies in, all flutter and flash,
weakening wing that quivers and finally
        grows still. A glitch in the way of things,
beauty arrested where by design
        it should have flown. Eight legs gingerly
touch feathers, regard the onyx eye.

Night Crawlers

Slick moonbathers come out to work
on the glisten, the soap-bubble
sheen of their backs—to find each other,
hermaphroditic, perfect
exchange, bodies side by side,
expanding and contracting.
Let's try: the lengths of us
touching. No lungs, they breathe
through moistened skin.
No eyes, they flinch from light,
slide into the forgiving underground.
Close your eyes. Everything that falls
passes through, clarified.
We have seen it, simplicity
splayed on the dissection table,
that long, untroubled line.
When someday they find us
in the fragrant loam of their castings,
they will take us in, lend us
the length of their generous symmetry,
all five soft pulsing hearts.

A Girl Restored to Life
Mark 5:21–43

What had faded
growing again distinguishable,
like the distant approach of a crowd:
galaxy of voices, bright
points of sound, coalescing, someone
touching the shape of my hand —
the weight of it, a shadow I'd left
on my mother's breast.
A voice so close I feel
its heat against my ear: *Talitha kum.*
Little girl, — what I am — *get up.*
Eyes unready for the glare, fingers
reaching for the smooth wood
sides of the cot, the beautiful
grain of it. Toes first
to meet the cool packed earth, then
balls of my feet, then heels. Knees,
thighs, hips press up like a breath.
Tomorrow I'll be twelve, and here
I am, in a body, this one,
every hair tingling,
the wool blanket rough and warm
across my shoulders. The smell,
damp sheep and my own sweat.
My own palms on my chest,
the shock of skin to skin.

Recipe for Resurrection

Just add water
from the River Jordan,
from the Mississippi,
from the rock's dry mouth.
Turn wine into water
and drink it.
Look up from the road-killed hawk
to its mirror, circling.
Add buzzard breath,
worm casting, cicada skin.
Sing the doxology backward.
Collect sap weeping
from ice-broke boughs —
turn water into sugar
and drink it.
Just add snake skin,
starfish arm, dung beetle.
Cut the nets, throw
back the fish.
Go back to Galilee.
Bottle the fog from the valley bottom
before it lifts.
Drink it.
Follow the honey bee
to the body of the lion.
Forgive, forgive, forgive.

Winter Wren

There are birds I've heard and never seen,
voices rising like a cold spring.

A wink of wings. The rest obscured
in trembling leaves. Struck, I tried

to notate descending triplets,
then ascending, an eighth rest, a tone

of indiscernible length,
so melodic and yet—erasing, listening,

hearing differently each time—
I couldn't get it right.

Like the time I dreamed of bluebirds for a week,
flying into my face, flutter of summer

sky, pale blaze of rusty breast,
then gone so fast I didn't know

which way to find them.
Sometimes there was only

a clearing, bright blue feathers strewn—
or laid—about the floor. As though

I'd stumbled on a threshold,
and didn't know if I should cross.

Things would be different if I were the girl
who befriends the cuckoo bird

that every hour comes out of a clock door
and takes her with him, slipping through

some thin place into layers
of hidden worlds. No one ever believes you

when you come back from such a place.

Epithalamion

The elm weaves the field's late light, this hill
hanging from the tree's roots like the moon
from its shadow and the whole
world beneath suspended.

Roots knead the earth's thick sorrow.
Still, leaves from this.
From this unshackling, birdsong.

I am a blade of corn where you kneel,
wind and quaking stalk.
The elm's body a vase of poured sky.

The tree will die.
Someday, the tree will die.

For now, this axis—
what we choose to compass by.

Manna, Honeydew

Ravenous little angels of hunger,
insects crawling the desert by night,
scale, coccid, parasites of our Lord, eat
for the sake of our starving hearts,
weak and abraded, raw with doubt—
suck, for the sake our emptiness, the sweet
phloem sap of what green fronds dare
root here. Turn it, in the hidden path
of your singular intestine
to the grace of our each morning:
the shit of seraphim our sustenance,
kicked back and scattered, a fine frost
melting in midday sun. Or, on the tongue,
as wafers made with honey, white
        seed of coriander.

Notes

"The Svalbard Global Seed Vault": The seed vault is located deep inside a sandstone mountain on Norway's Spitsbergen Island, above the Arctic Circle. Though its purpose is to preserve biodiversity and act as a backup to other gene banks, it has been nicknamed a "doomsday vault." It could preserve most of the world's major food crops' seeds for hundreds of years, some for thousands.

"The Artist's Studio in an Afternoon Fog": Winslow Homer's mother was a painter as well. Henry James commented of Homer, "He naturally sees everything at one with its envelope of light and air."

"The Berry Pickers": Winslow Homer is thought to have said, "Artists should never look at pictures, but should stutter in a language of their own."

"Golden Orb": Simon Peers and Nicholas Godley built a machine (based on one built by French missionary Jacob Paul Camboué in the 1880s) that can extract silk from two dozen spiders at once without harming them. Over the course of four years, they extracted enough silk—80 feet from each of more than a million golden orb weaver spiders collected from telephone polls in Madagascar—to weave a stunning, golden, 11-foot by 4-foot textile. Once the wild spiders were "milked," they were released.

"Manna": Many scholars believe that the exiled Israelites' manna from heaven was actually insect excrement, known as "honeydew" and still gathered by desert nomads today.

Acknowledgments

I am grateful to the editors of the following publications in which some of these poems or earlier versions of them first appeared: *Alaska Quarterly Review, Calyx, Catamaran, Drunken Boat, The Cortland Review, faultline, Grist, Hawk & Handsaw, The Massachusetts Review, MassPoetry.org, Mead, PMS, Rhino, Terrain.org, Water~Stone Review,* and *upstreet.*

Many thanks to the teachers who have made all the difference, especially Cleopatra Mathis, Eleanor Wilner, and Rick Barot.

To the friends and fellow writers who gave their time and attention to these poems to help them be the best they could be: Michelle Gillett, Patty Crane, Nina Ryan, Chris Dombrowski, Liz Goodman, and all my Warren Wilson classmates.

To my insightful and generous editor, Diana Gordon.

To my amazing parents and fabulous family. And, of course, to Adam.

HANNAH FRIES graduated from Dartmouth College and received an MFA in poetry from Warren Wilson College. From 2005 to 2014 she worked as an editor at *Orion* magazine in Great Barrington, Massachusetts. The recipient of a Bread Loaf scholarship and a Colorado Art Ranch residency, she currently works as a project editor at Storey Publishing in North Adams, Massachusetts, and is a contributing editor for Terrain.org.